Susan's Showy

Crochet Flower Patterns

Crochet Patterns for Beautiful and Bold Flowers

and Fun Drawstring Bag

Copyright 2015 Susan D. Kennedy

The pattern designs in this book are original and protected by copyright. Please do not copy or distribute them in any manner, electronic or physical. However, designers and crafters both online and in physical settings may feel free to make and sell items created from these patterns, with full permissions. Attribution is appreciated.

Susan's Showy Crochet Flower Patterns

Crochet Patterns for Beautiful and Bold Flowers and Fun Drawstring Bag

by Susan Kennedy

Table of Contents:

Notes and Materials………………………………………………………………………...4

Terms and Abbreviations used in this Pattern Set ………………………………………...5

Large Natural Rose ………………………………………………………………………..6

Sassy Zinnia ……………………………………………………………………………....14

Peony……………………………………………………………………………….……..19

From-the-Outside-In One Piece Zinnia …………………………………………….....…23

Baby Button Peony ……………………………………………………………..……….29

Sassy Spring Flower …………………………………………………………………..…37

Swirly Flower #1 ……………………………………………………………………...…42

Swirly Flower #2……………………………………………………………………….…44

Susan's Simple One-Piece Rose Pattern …………………………………………………46

Cool Cotton Thread Crochet Flower ……………………………………………………..51

Susan's Loopy Flower …………………………………………………………………....52

New Mum II ……………………………………………………………………………..57

Ruffled Flower I …………………………………………………………………………65

Ruffled flower II …………………………………………………………………………69

Simple Drawstring Flower Bag …………………………………………………………..75

3

Notes and Materials

This new collection of crochet flower patterns is a set of fourteen of my latest: crocheted flowers which are bulky, showy and different! Some are large, some are small, but all are intended to punch up a scarf, purse or hairstyle with a homespun flower that has power! Dive into the whole pile with all of your scrap yarns, medium or light weight, it doesn't matter! **If you use medium weight yarns (#4), most of these flowers will work best with a size G or H hook.** (4.25mm or 5.0 mm) **For a lightweight yarn (#3), choose a D or E hook** (3.25mm or 3.5 mm).

Work up a whole garden of lovely flowers and scatter them everywhere!

These instructions are for the intermediate crocheter. **You will need to know these stitches:** single crochet, double crochet, triple crochet, chain stitch, slip stitch, and in some of the patterns an optional stitch called a long single crochet stitch (this is also called a "spike stitch," and there are many helpful YouTube videos - including mine - about how to do it. Search YouTube for "VideoLongSingleCrochet" and you will find mine.) A few of the flowers also use the technique of working a stitch in only one of the previous stitch's loops. This is very easy, and when you see "FLO" or "BLO", you will know to work a stitch in the "front loops only" or "back loops only."

Have a great time with your crochet!

Terms and Abbreviations used in these Patterns

Beg *beginning* (as in, "sc in beg chain" – *single crochet in the chain at the beginning of this portion*).

BLO *back loops only*; work your stitch in only the back loop of the top of a stitch.

Ch *chain*

Dc *double crochet*

FLO *front loops only*; work you stitch in only the front loop of the top of a stitch.

Hdc *half double crochet* - a stitch in which you yarn over as in dc, but after inserting your hook, you yarn over again and take all loops off your hook at once like a sc, instead of in two stages as in dc. This makes a stitch which is slightly bulkier than a sc, therefore just a bit taller, for design purposes.

Lsc *long single crochet*, in which the hook is inserted below the normal space, to a previous round, resulting in a very long post which covers previous single crochets and double crochets (depending on the situation). Search youtube.com for "VideoLongSingleCrochet" and you should be able to see my explanation in video form.

Picot *A picot is a small decorative bump* made by making a chain, then going back to a loop a few chains back (the pattern determines how many), inserting your hook, yarning over and pulling through a sl st to join and form the bump

Prev *previous*

Rnd *round*

Sc *single crochet*

Sep *separated*

Sl st *slip stitch* (running your thread through some work to get to a new place without changing the shape of the work; or, attaching to a stitch with just a loop pulled through)

Sp *space* formed in your work, usually on a previous round

Tc *triple crochet* (similar to a double stitch, but worked with 3 initial yarn-over loops, not two, making the stitch a three-part stitch process, not two. This results in a taller stitch.

Flower Patterns:

Large Natural Rose

Above: natural rose worked in Caron Simply Soft yarn ("Strawberry") and a size K hook (rose is approximately 3" across)

Large Natural Rose worked in various yarns

This simple but beautiful rose is worked primarily in single and double crochet. It's worked in two pieces: first you will work the circular sc base for the rose, then you will work the petals of the rose right on to the stitches of this sc circle. This is an easy and super quick rose, with discrete petals spiraling gracefully out from the center. It will work up to approximately 3 inches across to make a big splashy decoration for your baby hat, when worked in medium weight yarn and a size K hook; for a smaller and more delicate rose use baby weight yarn and a size G hook.

Instructions for Rose

First work your circular base:

Rnd 1: Ch 2, work 6 sc in 2nd loop from hook.

Rnd 2: Continue on without joining (working in a spiral), working 2 sc in back loop only of every stitch of rnd
1. do not join, but continue in your spiral:

Rnd 3: work (sc, 2sc) in back loop only of stitches of rnd 2: 18 sc (in other words, sc around,

working an inc in every other st. Do not join, but continue:

Rnd 4: work (sc, sc, 2sc) in back loop only of stitches of rnd 3: 24 sc (in other words, sc around, working an inc in every other st. Go on to work (sc, sc, 2 sc) once mote: circle of 25 sc. Sl st in next st and tie off. Base finished. You will notice that your base circle is cupped somewhat, which will help to hold your rounds of petals beautifully, since you can "pop" it from the inside to let your rose pose nicely.

Now you will start building those spiraling petals all in one round, working on the circular base. Attach your yarn close to the center of your sc base, onto the innermost front loop of your sc work that you can find. (See photo below)

Before you start on petals, note that your work will stand up vertically from the base it is worked on, so you may wish to fold your base back to facilitate working on these spiraling front loops. In the instructions below "loop" refers to these remaining front loops from your sc's of your circular rose base.

Rnd 5: Petal Rounds which are worked in a spiral from the inside of your circle outward: Work ch 1, sc in first loop. Ch 1, dc in same loop, dc in each of next 4 loops, ch 1, sl st in same loop. *First petal made. See photo below.*

Continue in same direction:

Work sl st in next loop, ch 1, *[(3 dc, tc) in same st, work decr dc in next 2 loops](first ruffle or "scallop" of this petal made), repeat from * once- this adds a second scallop - then ch 1, sl st in same loop. *Second petal, consisting of two scallops, made. See photo below.*

9

Continue on in this round to form a third rose petal:

Work sl st in next loop, ch 1, *[(3 dc, tc) in same st, work decr dc in next 2 loops] (first scallop of third petal made), repeat from * twice - this adds two more scallops - then ch 1, sl st in same loop. *Third petal, consisting of three scallops, made. See photo below.*

Continue on to form a fourth rose petal: (not pictured)

Work sl st in next loop, ch 1, *[(3 dc, tc) in same st, work decr dc in next 2 loops] (first scallop of fourth petal made), repeat from * three times - this adds three more scallops - then ch 1, sl st in same loop. Fourth petal, consisting of three scallops, made. Continue on to form a fifth rose petal:
Work sl st in next loop, ch 1, *[(3 dc, tc) in same st, work decr dc in next 2 loops] (first scallop of fifth petal made), repeat from * four times - this adds four more scallops - then ch 1, sl st in

10

same loop. Fifth petal, consisting of five scallops, made. Continue on to form the final petal:

Work sl st in next loop, ch 1, (3 dc, tc) in same st, work decr dc in next 2 loops, (first scallop of last petal made), then work (3 tc in next loop, decr tc in next 2 loops) 3 times, 3 dc in next loop, sc in last loop, tie off and weave ends through work OR work a rose leaf (I don't use this leaf when I attach a rose to a hat, but I do like it when using the rose for an embellishment on a purse, scarf or hair tie).

Optional leaf:

Continuing on with your yarn from the rose petal rounds:

Work 7 ch, (see photo below)

11

turn, work sc in 2nd ch from hook, then work sc, dc in next ch, 2 dc in each of next 2 ch, dc, sc (see photo on next page),

ch 1, then pass over the ch-7 "vein" of leaf to continue in counter-clockwise fashion working stitches on other side of chain foundation:

Work ch 1, sc, dc, 2 dc, 2 dc, dc, sc in chain foundation, then ch 1 join to tip of leaf. Now you will surface crochet back down center of leaf to its base where it meets the rose (see photo on next page).

Tie off and weave end through work.

13

Sassy Zinnia

This small flower is quick and easy, tight and dense. You'll love it on a small child's project which needs a durable embellishment.

For the Center of the flower, use a lightweight yarn or a cotton thread or fine yarn like you see in the collections Lion Brand makes in its "Bon Bons" variety packs at craft stores. For the center use a size E or F hook; For the rest of the flower you can use a light or medium weight yarn with an F or G hook.

Center:
Ch 5, join to form small ring.

Rnd 1: Work 8 sc OVER the chains of the ring just formed. If desired, repeat this for a chunkier center ring. Join to blo of beg st of round.

Continue on to work in a spiral, no joining, working in back loops only (BLO) of sc's from this point: work (sc, 2 sc) around twice, until you have a circle of 19 sc. Sl st in next sc and tie off.

Rnd 2: attach to first loop on your flower base which splits off from inner sc ring (see photo)

Ch 2, 2 dc,ch 2, sl st, all in same st.. Continue on to work *(sl st in back loop only of next sc, ch 2, 2dc,ch 2, sl st, all in same st,

16

repeat from * around until you reach last rnd of sc (after 14 petals). Your petals will be crowded.

From that point work double size petals in every other loop: sl st in next st, *ch3, 2tc, ch3, sl st in NEXT st, sl st in next st,

17

repeat from * for a total of 10 petals. Tie off and weave ends through back side of work.

Peony

This peony is more challenging than some of the other flowers in this book, not because any of the stitches are hard, but because it is larger and takes a little more time with that final round of large floppy petals. But the same difficulty is what makes it one of the showiest.

I like to work this flower in four colors, color #1, usually a pale green for the center disk, color #2 for the inner stamens, color #3 for the inner rings of petals, and color #4 for the outermost ring of large petals. If you want a smaller peony, perhaps 4" across, use a light weight yarn and a size E hook. For a larger peony (5 to 5 ½"), use medium weight yarns and a size G or H hook. I haven't broken this flower down into rounds because much of it is worked in a spiral and it seemed better to categorize the round by flower part.

Circular Base for Flower: In color # 1 (pale green in example), start a disc of sc: ch 1, tighten to form a small knot (this is optional, and helps prevent loosening); ch 2, work 6 sc in 2nd loop from hook, and, working in back loops only, start working in a spiral with no joining: 2 sc in each sc 18 times: circle of 24 sc, with front loops visible and forming a spiral from the inside out. These will be the loops you form your petals on in the instructions below.

Continue working on your circular base, forming chains and spokes which will be the outer edge of your circular base, still working in back loops only:

Sl st in next sc,*(ch 5, turn, skip 1st ch, sc in next 3 ch, ch 1, skip over next 2 sc of disc, sl st in back lp of next sc of disc) repeat from * around, join, tie off. You will have a circle of sc ringed with 8 spokes.

Stamens and Petals: Attach color # 2 (pale pink in example below) to centermost front loop of sc in base. Work 6 stamens: * ch 2, turn, skip 1st ch, work 3 sc in next ch and sc in next front loop of base sc, repeat from
* 5 times, leaving off last sc and joining to first ch of this rnd.

20

Sl st in next loop of spiral and change to color # 3 if desired (a variegated pink medium weight yarn in example).

Continue working in spiral fashion to create the cupped petals of peony: * ch 3, work 3 dc tog in the same loop and next 2 loops, then picot – this is a ch 2, join to 2nd loop from hook to make a small bump – then continue on to ch 3, sl st in same loop of base, sl st in next loop, repeat 10 times; (see photo below)

and work these cupped petals out till you reach the chained spokes of outer edge of base disc. You should have 11 cupped petals. (Don't worry if the number varies!)

At the end of the sc's and the beg of the loops and spokes of chains change to color #4

21

(dark pink in example), working *sc in sp at beg of next spoke, then work 3 dc in ea of next 2 ch , 3 dc at the st at the tip of the spoke, and 3 dc also in each of the last two sc of the far side of the spoke, then work sc in sp after spoke. Repeat from * 7 times for 8 large petals.

Tie off and weave yarn ends through the back of your work.

From-the-Outside-In One Piece Zinnia

The examples above are worked in a medium weight yarn for the main color, a lightweight yarn for the last few stitches of the flower center. Use a size G hook – for the medium weight yarn - and D hook – for the lightweight yarn.

Create a flat sc circle for flower base: work in Front Loops Only!
Rnd 1 of base: Ch 2, work 6 sc in 2nd ch from hook. Continue working in the round in the same direction, no joining:

Rnd 2 of base: work 2 sc in FLO of every sc around, do not join: 12 sc circle

Rnd 3 of base: in FLO work (sc, 2 sc) around, do not join: 18 sc circle

Rnd 4 of base: in FLO work (sc, sc, 2 sc) around. (See photos below) Sl st in next st, and flip to reverse side of work

After Rnd 4

Flip to reverse side of work and notice the spiral of left-over loops into which you will work your next stitches.

First outer petal round is a round of tc petals in every other stitch: Ch 3, tc in 1st (outermost) sc of circle, ch 3, sl st in same sc, *skip next sc, sl st in next sc, (ch 3, tc, ch 3, sl st in same sc), repeat from * around the outermost sc's of the circle. (See photo below).

At the end of the round, you should have 12 petals. Do not turn (do not flip), or join, but continue on in the same direction:

As you reach the point where the sc's spiral inward, insert your hook in the remaining back loop of the next sc of the base circle (see photo on next page)

Now you have finished the outer petals and will start spiraling inward, continuing to work in the round.

Work a round of dc petals in every loop: sl st, ch 2, dc in same loop, ch 2, sl st in same loop, *sl st in next loop, (ch 2, dc, ch 2, sl st in same loop), repeat from * for eighteen somewhat crowded dc petals. (This is one round around the center).

Next, a round of dc petals in every other loop: *skip next loop, sl st in next loop, (ch 2, dc, ch 2, sl st in same loop), repeat from * for six petals (one round). This should leave you 6 loops, close to the center.

In these rounds it is helpful to fold down the base disc so you can more easily work in these loops from the first rnd of the flower.

You will stop when you reach the last 6 loops of the inward spiral, change color to a lightweight white or pale green or yellow, (dmc embroidery floss is great for flower centers: I have used # 165). Also switch to a smaller D hook) and work as follows:

*(sl st, ch 7, sl st) in next loop, repeat from * 5 times, tie off.

Pull all, yarn or thread ends through to back of flower and weave through work.

Baby Button Peony

Above: Baby Button Peony. The yellow and green examples have the optional extra dc described in round 8, which make them slightly fuller.

For this showy flower, use a light weight ("baby" or "sport" weight) yarn and a size E (3.5mm) aluminum crochet hook. Your flower should measure approximately 3" across. You can also make a larger and chunkier flower using a typical medium weight ("worsted") yarn and a size H (5.0mm) hook.

Center:

Rnd 1: ch 1, tighten loop to form a small knot (this is optional, but keeps your center from loosening). Ch 3, work 9 dc in 3rd ch from hook. Join to top of beg ch 3.

Rnd 2: Inserting your hook way down into the center of your circle, work 18 long single crochet stitches all the way around your circle, covering it with this puffy stitch. If you can get to youtube on a computer or phone, you can search for "VideoLongSingleCrochet" and you should be able to find my video explanation of this stitch.

Above: Insert your hook into the center of your dc ring

30

Above: How your finished flower center of 18 lsc stitches will look

Rnd 3: Work a round of 18 chained loops in front loops only (flo) of rnd 2 stitches: in flo, work *(ch 4, sl st in next st), repeat from * around, join. Ch 1.

Your loops will be crowded and fluffy, for a first round of "stamens"

Next: if desired, change to a contrasting color (pink in the example). If changing colors, attach to first loop on back side of flower.

Rnd 4: Reach back to these back loops of the lsc stitches from rnd 2, and work a round of sc: sc in every loop of the 18 back loops from rnd 2, join. (See photo below of the back side of your work)

Rnd 5: Now work a round of small petals: Sc in flo of 1st sc, *Ch 2, dc in flo of same sc and in flo of next sc, ch 2, sc in flo of same st, sc in flo of next st, repeat from * around, join to base of first petal of this rnd: 9 small petals (see photo below)

Above: a view of rnd 5 from the back

Above: a view of rnd 5 from the front

Rnd 6: Reach back to back side of flower, ch1, sl st in blo of remaining loop from rnd 4, *ch 3, skip 2 sc, sc in next blo of next sc, repeat from * around, join at base of first sc: 6 ch 3 loops.(see photo below)

The last two rounds will be your larger outside petals, and they will consist of two rounds.

Note on round 8 that you can add an extra dc for a slightly more ruffled petal. (the yellow and green flowers in the main photo are examples of this)

Rnd 7: You will be working stitches onto the ch 3 loops just formed: In ch 3 loop *sc, ch 2, 4 dc, ch 2, sc in same loop, sc in next loop, repeat from * around, do not join: 6 small petals (see photo below)

Rnd 8: Second round which is worked on top of the small petals just formed: *sc in first sc from rnd 7, ch 2, dc in ch 2 sp, (see photo below),

dc in next dc, 3 dc in ea of next 2 dc, **(OR for a more ruffled petal option, work 4 dc in each of the next 2 dc),** dc in next dc, dc in next ch 2 sp, ch 2, sc in sc, repeat from * around. Join and tie off. Weave yarn end through the back side of your work.

Sassy Spring Flower

Experiment with different materials for this flower! For a large, mostly yarn flower, I like medium weight yarns in white and three or four contrasting colors; I add a strand of black crochet thread to the center of the flower, and I also have another contrast color of crochet thread for the edging. Use a size G crochet hook for most of the parts, and a size 6 steel thread crochet hook for the optional embroidery floss edging.

Center of Flower:

Rnd 1: This will be a small circle of dc. Use one of your bright yarn colors, and, if you wish, hold a strand of crochet thread (black in the example) and use the two strands as one.
Ch 3, join to 3rd ch from hook to form a tiny ring, then work 2 ch, dc 11 times in ring to form a small disc. Join and tie off. Weave end through back of work.

Rnd 2: work 20 long single crochet stitches over the dc's from prev round; these stitches will be crowded, but the number is needed for your petal rounds!

Your center after the long single crochet stitches

If you're not sure how to work a long single crochet, just remember that a long single crochet stitch is the same as a normal single crochet, except that you insert your hook in a different place. In the case of this circular flower center, you'll be inserting your hook into the center of the circle of dc's. Then you'll yarn over, adjust your tension so that the working thread isn't too loose or tight, and finish your crochet stitch as if it were a normal single crochet. If you would like to see a video explaining this, search youtube for "VideoLongSingleCrochet" and my small tutorial should appear in the results.

Contrasting center ring of flower:

You can either make this decorative round of 20 simple single crochet stitches, or ten small groups of 2 sc worked in every other lsc stitch of the central disc.

Contrasting center ring, 20 stitch version: (see example above) Attach second bright color to your disc. Ch 1, work sc in every lsc around, join and tie off. Weave end through back of work.

Contrasting center ring, 10 cluster version: (see example below): Attach second bright color to your disc. Ch 1, work 2 sc in every other lsc around, join and tie off. Weave end through back of work.

Petals: attach white yarn to your work and work a total of 5 7- dc petals separated by 5 sc's, as indicated in the following directions:

Ch 1, *skip next 2 sc, work 7 dc in next sc, skip 2 sc, sc in next sc, repeat from * around, join to ch 1 from beg of rnd. Tie off and weave end through the back of your work.

Optional Decorative Chained Round:

This round (see the green chains being worked in the photo above) is simply working chain stitches across your work to make a decorative round of stitches. You can either work these chains around the outer edge of the contrasting round of sc's, or around the outer edge of the lsc's from the center of the flower.

Draw your strand of bright color #3 through to the front of your flower so that you have a small loop on your crochet hook; then insert your hook in the next stitch and pull the working yarn from the back to the front for a chain stitch which skips across the top of your work as shown in the photo above. When you reach your beginning point, join, tie off and weave your end through the back of your work.

Optional decorative edging:
For a bright edge to your white yarn petals, experiment with adding a round of sc's in embroidery floss or colored crochet thread. (see photo below) You can still use your size G hook, or switch to a size 6 steel thread crochet hook for a tighter look, and work as follows.

Attach thread to any petal at its low point. Work sc in every dc, and if desired, work a lsc at the top of every petal and in the mid-points between every petal (see photo below) . Join at beginning point, tie off and weave end through the back of your work.

Note on edging: Another option is to vary this edging by working 2 sc in every stitch instead of one, as written.)

Swirly Flower #1

Work these little flowers in three of your colors, color #1 for the flower center (yellow in example), color #2 for the petals (orange in example), and color #3 for the spiral, stem and leaf (green in example).

Center: In color #1 (yellow in example)
Ch 1, tighten to form a small knot (this is optional, and serves to tighten your work so it doesn't come loose). Ch 2, work 6 sc in 2nd ch from hook; continuing on in a spiral (not joining), work on top of your first 6 stitches, working 2 sc in every sc for next 6 st; then continuing in your spiral, work 2 sc in every other sc for the third round, ending with 18 sc in your circle. Sl sl in next sc, then break away from the center to chain 20 times (for the standard height flower - make it 30 chains for a tall flower), tie off. You'll have a plain "lollipop" of stitches.

Petals: attach color #2 (orange in example) at base of flower where center meets stem and work small shells: *skip 1 st, work 4 dc shell in next st, sc in next st, repeat from * around: 6 4-dc shells. Tie off.

Decorative Spiral, Stem and Leaf: attach color #3 (green in example)
Edge with surface crochet as before (on your chameleon), beginning the chains by pulling up a loop through the center of the spiral and working chains across the surface of your work, following the sc's around in a counterclockwise spiral until you reach the stem. Then continue on

to sl st halfway down stem, then work Optional leaf:

Ch 6, turn, skip 1st ch at tip of leaf, sl st in next ch, sc in ch, dc in ch, sc in ch, skip across foundation ch-6 at its point of origin, and work back toward tip of leaf on the other side of the foundation chains: sc, dc, sc, ch 1, join to tip, turn to surface crochet down center of leaf to form vein. When you reach stem turn and continue to sl st down the last part of the stem to its end. Tie off and knot securely.

Swirly Flower #2

Work this spiky little flower in three of your colors, color #1 for the flower center (orange in example), color #2 for the petals (blue in example), and color #3 for the spiral, stem and leaf (green in example).

Center: In color #1 (orange in example)
Ch 1, tighten to form a small knot (this is optional, and serves to tighten your work so it doesn't come loose). Ch 2, work 6 sc in 2nd ch from hook; continuing on in a spiral (not joining), work on top of your first 6 stitches, working 2 sc in every sc for next 6 st; then continuing in your spiral, work 2 sc in every other sc for the third round, ending with 18 sc in your circle. Sl sl in next sc, then break away from the center to chain 20 times (for the standard height flower - make it 30 chains for a tall flower), tie off. Like Swirly Flower #1, you'll have a plain "lollipop" of stitches at this point.

Petals: attach color #2 (blue in example) at base of flower where center meets stem and work small triangles:

*(sc, dc, ch 1, skip last ch, join to last dc - picot formed) in next sc, (dc, sc) in next sc, repeat from * around for a ring of 9 pointed small petals.

Spiral, Stem and Leaf: attach color #3 (green in example)

Edge with surface crochet as before (on your chameleon), beginning the chains by pulling up a loop through the center of the spiral and working chains across the surface of your work, following the sc's around in a counterclockwise spiral until you reach the stem. Then continue on to sl st halfway down stem, then work Optional leaf:

ch 6, turn, skip 1st ch at tip of leaf, sl st in next ch, sc in ch, dc in ch, sc in ch, skip across foundation ch-6 at its point of origin, and work back toward tip of leaf on the other side of the foundation chains: sc, dc, sc, ch 1, join to tip, turn to surface crochet down center of leaf to form vein. When you reach stem, turn and continue to sl st down the last part of the stem to its end. Tie off and knot securely.

Susan's Simple One-Piece Rose Pattern

I love this particular rose pattern because it's formed all in one piece which (for me) makes it more enjoyable and meditative. Once you get used to making it, you'll be making them one after another!

You get around the necessity of a flat base to work on by creating a base or foundation round of sc in every other round. The pattern is: base round, petal round, base round, petal round, etc. etc. Pay attention to the notes about when to work in front loops only and when to work in back loops only!

Rnd 1: Ch 2, dc 9 times in ring, join. (see photo below)

Rnd 2: (This is the center petal shape which stands up vertically, since it will be crocheted in the **front loops only** from rnd 1) Ch 2, working in front loops only, work *(decr dc in next 3 dc, -in other words, work 3 dc's together- see photo below, and also refer to the abbreviations section of this pattern for additional instructions on decr dc)

5 dc in next dc) , repeat once from *, dc, do not join. You will have a curvy set of dc's, some decreases and some increases, which stand up from the center disc.

Rnd 3: (This is a round of sc which "grows" the base disc on which the petals are formed) Ch 1, reach back to work in back loops only of same dc's from rnd 1- see photo below:

47

work *(sc in dc, 2 sc in next dc) repeat from * around, join to the back loop of the first sc of this rnd: 13 stitches
(if you have one more or one less, just plow ahead, it's not going to matter!)
This is how your center petal and the next foundation round of sc's from round 3 will look at the end of round 3: a curved rosebud shape standing up on that base disc. (photo below)

Rnd 4: *(This is the second ruffly petal)* Ch 2, then working in **front loops only** (see photo below) of sc's from prev rnd, work *(2 dc in sc, 3 dc in next sc) , repeat from *around, join to second ch of this rnd.

48

Below see a photo of the rose as it looks after the end of this second ruffled round (round 4):

Rnd 5: *(Next round of base disc)* ch 2, reach back to work in back loops only of sc's from rnd 3, (see photo below) work *(sc in sc, 2 sc in next sc) , repeat from * around, join to the back loop of the first sc of this rnd.

Rnd 6: *(Third ruffly petal)* Ch 2, then working in front loops only of sc's from prev rnd, work *(2 dc in sc, 3 dc in next sc) , repeat from * around, join to front loop of first dc of this rnd.

Repeat rnds 5 and 6, then join and tie off. (this last sc round and ruffle not shown.) Weave end through work. The finished rose is shown below:

50

Cool Cotton Thread Crochet Flower

*I use this with a "Cool Cotton Baby Hat" pattern of mine which is worked with two strands of crochet thread and a size G hook **instead** of baby yarn. The cotton crochet thread is, to me, much cooler for your baby, and it's an option you can use with many (or most) baby hat patterns. Try it, and see if it doesn't turn your typical baby hat into a nice summer beach hat. All that to say, work this flower with doubled up strands of no. 10 cotton crochet thread and a size G crochet hook (4.25 mm). If you don't want to use two strands of crochet thread, feel free to make this flower with lightweight yarn and a G hook!*

Center:
Start with a double strand of main body colors of hat.
Rnd 1: Disc of 14 dc OR cover a disc of 10 dc with 14 lsc.

First Ring of Petals:
In front loops only of 14 stitches from the center, work as follows: Attach double strand of white.
Rnd 2: Work 7 petals in every other stitch: *(sc, ch 1, 4 dc, ch 1, sc, skip next stitch), repeat from * around: 7 petals. Slip stitch to 1st back loop of 1st st from rnd 1, then work 7 more petals directly behind first 7:
Rnd 3: work *(sc, ch 1, 4 dc, ch 1, sc, skip next st), repeat from * around. Rnd 4: continue on for a second rnd which makes the rnd 3 petals larger:
Sl st at base of first petal, * ch 2, - counts as 1st dc - dc in 1st dc of petal, dc in each of next 2 dc, 2 dc in last dc, ch 2, sc at base of same petal, sc at base of next petal, repeat from * around. Tie off and weave ends through work.

Susan's Loopy Flower

This full and showy flower works up to approximately 3 1/2" across when using a medium weight yarn and a size H (5.00 mm) crochet hook, smaller if you use a baby yarn and a size G hook. It looks a lot like the "Cool Cotton Thread Crochet Flower, but the "petals" are simply loops of chains, which makes it a bit simpler to work.

Center of Flower:
Rnd 1: Ch 3, join to form small ring. Ch 2, dc 10 times in ring. Join.

Rnd 2: Cover dcs of rnd 1 with 16 long single crochet stitches. (see photo below)

(Again, search youtube for "VideoLongSingleCrochet" if you'd like a little tutorial). Do not join, but continue on in a spiral:

Rnd 3: work (2 sc, sc) around, working in BLO (back loops only): 24 sc.(see photo on next page)

Rnd 4: Reach inward to the remaining loops from rnd 2 and work in them:

*sc in next loop from rnd 2, ch 8, repeat from * around, join: you should have 16 ch-8 loops.

Do not join but continue working in the round:
Rnd 5: now work more ch-8 loops in the scs from rnd 3:

work *sc in next sc, ch8, repeat from * around, join: 16 ch-8 loops.

Sew this sweet flower to the side of your baby hat, to a scarf, purse or slipper for a fun and cheerful accent!

New Mum II

*This full and showy chrysanthemum can be worked in any weight yarn with its suggested hook size; but I prefer a **medium weight yarn and a size F or G** for a nice tight stitch...**or a light weight (baby weight) yarn with a size D** or E hook. If you use a soft and flexible yarn, its petals will curl more, as in the blue and gray mums in the photo above. A more sturdy acrylic yarn will yield a flower with stiffer petals.*

*You can **choose either a button style center** (shown in the blue and grey example) **or a nubby center of sc** with small loops (shown in the white example)*

*Use **two colors of yarn**, one for the flower center, and one for the main color of your flower.*

In your first yarn color for your center, (I chose light green light weight yarns), make your flower center first, ending with a round of 18 stitches to build your mum petals on:

Button center:

Rnd 1: Ch 3, join to form small ring. Ch 2, dc 11 times in ring. Join.

Rnd 2: Cover dcs of rnd 1 with 18 long single crochet stitches. (You can see a small tutorial if you search youtube for "VideoLongSingleCrochet"). Join. ***Skip to Rnd 5 to complete your mum.***

Alternate Nubby Center:

Rnd 1: Ch 1, tighten to form a small knot (this is optional, but it keeps your work from loosening), then ch 2; in 2nd ch from hook work a sc circle of 6 sc (see photo on next page) Do not join.

Rnd 2: Work 2 sc in every sc: 12 sc.

Rnd 3: In FLO (front loops only), work *(sc, ch 3) in next sc, repeat from * around. (see photo on next page).

You will still have the remaining 12 back loops on the reverse side on which you will continue your flower (see photo on next page).

Rnd 4: In remaining back loops on reverse side, work (sc, 2 sc) around for a circle of 18 sc. (see photo below).

Change to main color of your flower (White in my example). Attach to ending point of last round.

Rnd 5: In FLO (front loops only) of last rnd, work *(ch 6, sc in next st), repeat from * around. Do not join.

Rnd 6: in remaining back loops *from Rnd 4*, work sc in every st. (see photo on next page) Do not join.

You will now work in the front loops only of the sc stitches just formed.

Rnd 7: *Sc in FLO of next sc,Ch 6, skip 1st ch and sc in next 5 ch back to center, repeat from * around. (see photos below) Do not join,

Side view of round 7

62

Front view of round 7- sc petals

Rnd 8: Again reach to back of flower and work next rnd in remaining back loops *from Rnd 6*:

Round 8 – dc petals

63

*Sc in next loop, Ch 8, skip 1st 2 ch, work dc in next 6 ch back to center, repeat from *around. See photo above. Join. Tie off and weave yarn end through the back of your work.
See how the back of your mum should look in the photo below).

(back view of mum)

And below see the finished Mum!

64

Ruffled Flower I

This sassy bold flower is a huge statement piece! Worked in medium weight yarn and a size G hook, it is fun and fairly simple to work. Start with the center, worked in color #1 (In my case, yellow)

Flower Center:
Rnd 1:Ch 1, tighten loop to form sm knot. ,ch2, work 6 sc in 2nd ch from hook. Join.

Rnd 2: work 6 loops: in FLO sc, *ch 5, sc, repeat 5 times, ending with join to first sc of rnd.

Rnd 3: Flip over to back side of flower. In BLO work ch 1,*sc in next remaining back loop from rnd 1,(ch 4, turn, skip 1st loop on hook,sc 3 times back to center, sc in same loop) 6 times, join to the base sc of the first of these 6 '"veins" for your petals to finish rnd.

Working rnd 3

After round 3

If desired, change to color #2 here.
Rnd 4: work on base "veins" just formed: work *ch 2, 2dc in first 2 sc of vein, work 4 dc in last sc,

First part of a round 4 petal

rotate counterclockwise to continue dcs in other side of vein:

Second part of a rnd 4 petal

4 dc, 2 dc, 2 dc, ch 2, sl st at base of last
dc worked, sl st in first st of next vein, repeat from * 5 times. Tie off and weave end through work.

Ruffled flower II

*This fun and different flower looks like a cheerful peony sitting on a child's hat or an Easter basket. I like to work it in three colors, using **medium weight yarn and a size F or G** for a nice tight stitch...**or a light weight (baby weight) yarn with a size D or E** hook.*

Center of Flower in Color # 1:

Rnd 1: Ch 1, tighten loop to form sm knot. Ch 3, work circle of 12 dc, join.

69

Rnd 2: Work decr sc around in all twelve sc of rnd 1:6 sc which cup inwards.

After rnd 2

Rnd 3: Change to color #2 if desired, work 2 sc in every sc, then continue on to work (sc, 2 sc)

70

for a round (total of 18 sc) join.

Rnd 4: (Rnd of 18 stamens):*(ch 5, sl st in flo of next st) around.

After Rnd 4

71

Change color. Flip over to back side of flower.

Rnd 5: In back loops only (BLO) which remain from the 18 sc, work: Ch 1, work rnd of sc:18 sc on back side of flower.

Back of flower after Rnd 5

Rnd 6: First rnd of ruffles: in FLO ch 2, *(3dc in sc, 3tc in sc)repeat around, join to top of first dc of rnd. Ch 2.

After rnd 6

Rnd 7 (2nd ruffle foundation):
This is a rnd of low ch-3 loops worked on remaining back loops from sc of rnd 5 (BLO). Sc in loop, *ch3, skip next sc, sc in sc, repeat from * around, join: 9 ch-3 loops.

After Rnd 7

Rnd 8: This is the second ruffle which will lay behind the first one.
Work ruffle in each loop: ch 2, *2dc,2tc,2dc all in next ch 3 loop, repeat from * around, join to first dc of rnd. Tie off and weave end through work.

74

Drawstring Flower Bag

This fun and easy little Drawstring Flower Bag is a perfect project for a beginning crocheter. It's also a sweet little gift for a child, an Easter basket alternative, a fun little giveaway, party favor or craft project holder! It costs you only the price of two bandanas and a few scrap bits of yarn, and costs nothing if you can scrounge a secondhand bandana, and have scrap yarn, a yarn needle and crochet hook on hand.

Each bag and flower can be made in 30 to 60 minutes depending upon your speed. The bag just has a circle of yarn stitches and a single round of crochet; the chained drawstring is a 45" long length of chains, and the flower is a few quick rounds of crochet. Weave your drawstring through your double crochet casing, sew on your flower, and you're done!

Materials for this pattern:

Two Bandanas or Hemmed Squares of Fabric, Store Bought or Secondhand (a square of fabric 22 inches on each side)

Steel Yarn or Tapestry Needle (with an eye large enough to accommodate medium weight yarn

Light Weight yarns (baby weight) in desired colors

Crochet Hook size size E (3.50 mm)

Scissors

Small Ruler and Pins, optional

Start with two 22" square bandanas or other (approximately 22" square) hemmed pieces of woven cotton cloth.

Next you will thread your yarn or tapestry needle with yarn and use a running stitch to create a large circle or rounded off square of yarn stitches on your bandana.

If you wish, draw a chalk circle or rounded off square on your bandanas which almost touches the sides of the squares. Or pin a paper circle or rounded square 2" from the edges of your bandanas. This will be a shape approximately 18" in diameter. It is also perfectly fine to stitch freehand, forming a circle of yarn stitches which is only an approximate circle: the imperfection of your circle shape will never be seen!

Pinning the rounded square shape where my yarn stitches will be

Step One: A circle (or rounded off square) of yarn stitches. Starting at a corner (So that the knotted ends will be well hidden under the flopping corner flap), use your yarn needle and a single strand of yarn to work a running stitch (make your stitches approximately ¼" long) which forms an outline just inside the outline of your bandana's edge. (see photo above). When your shape is complete, knot on the wrong side of the bandanas, and cut off ends at 1".

78

After step 1

Step Two: "Casing" for Chained Strap (the drawstring bag's string). This is a ladder-shaped round of crochet through which you will draw the string. Attach desired color of yarn to the same beginning point in your stitching. Tie the yarn end to your last stitch from the previous step. You'll be working a round of dc and chain stitches which will trace the same large circle, being worked on the base of the yarn stitches.

Work 4 ch (counts as first dc and ch), then dc in next yarn stitch, work *(ch 1, dc in next stitch), repeat from * around, join to 3rd ch of beg ch-4. Tie off and weave end through work.

(Below) This is how your bandana should look after your running stitch base and your round of chain/dc stitches are finished:

Step Three: Length of Chains for Drawstring Strap. Using a doubled up strand of yarn (or if you wish, even three strands of yarn), chain to a length of 45" or desired length.

When you are done, use a crochet hook or your yarn needle to weave this drawstring strap in and out through the posts of the double crochet stitches in your bag.

When you reach your beginning point, pull both ends of your chained strap out straight and knot them together at their ends.

To use your drawstring bag, just pull your circle shut with the strap, and sew on your crocheted flower! Enjoy!

Thanks for using my patterns! You can find more of my patterns on Amazon by searching for "Susan Kennedy crochet or you can visit www.susanlinnstudio.etsy.com Happy crocheting!

Printed in Great Britain
by Amazon